Advanced Business Principles: Strategic Management and Leadership

Arthur H Tafero

includes lesson plans

I0469141

Forward

   This text is designed for students in advanced levels of their business curriculum or for business owners who wish to apply the most professional principles to their business in order to achieve higher profit margins. The lesson plan outlines are broken down into two separate areas; one section in Strategic Management and another in Leadership.

   Strategic Manangement will include all of the earlier basic skills acquired in previous business courses including sales and marketing, organizational behavior, and measuring variables such as CPM (comparative profile matrix), SWOT (measuring strengths, weaknesses, opportunities and threats), OD (organizational diagnosis), IFE (Internal Factor Evaluation), EFE (External Factor Evaluation) and other Finance and Economic principles.

Arthur H Tafero

Table of Contents

Leadership Section

Tafero's Lesson Plans of Day - Strategic Management - Introduction - One

Lesson One – Introduction to Strategic Management

1. Strategic Management (Strategic Planning) 5 – art and science of formulating, implementing and evaluating cross functional decisions that enable an organization to achieve its objectives.
2. Alternative Definition of Strategic Management and Strategic Plan5 – Strategic Management is the formulation, implementation and evaluation of strategy, Strategic Plan is merely the strategic formulation.
3. Strategic Management Process 5 – Strategy Formulation, Strategy Implementation and Strategy Evaluation – This also includes coming up with Plan B, C, D and so on because PLAN A NEVER WORKS! (It cant because no one can even see one day into the future, so no plan ever works perfectly without knowledge of the future)
4. Strategy Formulation5 – developing a vision or mission, identifying external opportunities and threats (SWOT), determining internal strengths and weaknesses (SWOT), establishing objectives, generating alternative strategies, picking the best one, and preparing plans B, C, D and so on when this Plan A fails.
5. Strategy Implementation6 – action stage of plan
6. Strategy Evaluation 6 – Finding out whether your plan worked or not and 99.99% you will find out it did not work perfectly, therefore you have to make corrections for Plan B, C etc
7. Competitive Advantage8- Something you or your company does particularly better than others
8. Sustained Competitive Advantage 10 – continually adapting to maintain your edge in business
9. Vision Statement11 – What you want to become
10. Mission Statement11- The scope of a company's operations in product and market terms
11. SWOT – 12 – refers to internal strengths and weaknesses, opportunities and threats from outside
12. Objectives 13 – specific results an organization seeks to achieve
13. Strategies 13 – means by which a company attempts to achieve its objectives
14. Annual Objectives 13 – annual goals based on guesses by strategists; this are changed 100% of the time into Plan B, C and etc because no one can predict one day (much less one year) of event in the future.
15. Empowerment 17 – the act of giving employees more power
16. *****Advantages of Strategic Planning 18
a. Identifies opportunities
b. Examines management problems
c. Improves coordination
d. Improves control
e. It allocates time and work

f. It increases communication
g. It creates a team atmosphere
h. It develops discipline
17. Business Ethics21- principles of conduct within companies

ICA and HW Assignment – Lesson 1

HW 1 Essays –

1. Why is Strategic Management an essential business course?
2. Discuss the three basic elements of Strategic Management.
3. Discuss the advantages of Strategic Management
4. Discuss the Strategic Plan.

Internet Resources for this lesson:

General Reference Material For All Content

http://www.askmrmovies.com

Strategic Management

www.quickmba.com/strategy

Strategic Plan

www.managementhelp.org/plan_dec/str_plan/str_plan.htm

Tafero's Lesson Plans of the Day - Strategic Management - The Business Mission - Two

Lesson 2 – The Business Vision and Mission

*****1. Advantages of Creating a Mission Statement pg 59
a. It helps to unite the purpose of the organization
b. Creates a standard for allocating resources
c. Establishes the tone of the organizational climate
d. Serves as a focal point for employees
e. Translates objectives into the work structure
f. Cost, Time and Work can be measured and assessed to Mission Statement
*****2. Customer Marketing Advertising pg 66
a. Do not offer THINGS
b. Do not offer clothes, offer style and looks
c. Do not offer shoes, offer style and comfort
d. Do not offer a house, offer security, comfort, convenience, cleanliness
e. Do not offer a car, offer quality, sexual opportunity, and comfort
f. Do not offer books, offer knowledge and reading pleasure
g. Do not offer CDs, offer me relaxing or exciting music
h. Do not offer tools, offer the benefits of having tools, finished products
i. Do not offer furniture, offer comfort and style
j. Do not offer THINGS…offer ideas, emotions, ambience, feelings and benefits

3. The illusion of social responsibility by private companies
a. Often, private companies say one thing in their mission statements, but in actual practice, do quite the opposite.
b. Some mining companies often say how they improve life for people and provide jobs, but in reality, after they are finished stripping a mine, that land is ruined and all the people working in that area become unemployed. That does not sound too socially responsible to me.
c. Some banks say they are socially responsible in the community by donating small amounts of money to community efforts, but in reality, they will always favor the clients with the most money invested in their accounts with deals that dwarf the contributions they make to the community. They are aided by governments who also claim to be socially responsible, but these same governments (too numerous to mention) will often bail out a

billion dollar bank from bankruptcy and wipe out their debt....when was the last time a bank ever did that for you? (or a country)

d. Some companies highlight their wonderful pension plans to their retiring employees and then unprincipled officers of the company wipe out the pension funds with ill-advised investments in highly questionable stocks and real estate schemes. Case in point: ENRON

e. Some companies highlight the fact that their cosmetic products are environmentally safe and no threat to your health, but they do not mention that this same company had to torture hundreds of animals with their product to ensure these results.

f. Some companies in tech agree to allow countries to violate the individual rights of consumers in order to curry marketing advantages with the leaders of those countries.

g. There are SOME companies that are socially responsible, but certainly nowhere near the number that claim they are.

5. ****** Components of the Mission Statement page 70

a. Customers – Who are they (targeting)

b. Products or Services – What are you selling?

c. Markets – Demographics

d. Technology – Do you have a revenue-producing web site? No? Then you have no business; you have a low-end store.

e. Sustainability, Growth and Profit – if you don't sustain, you will perish, if you don't grow, you will get smaller, and if you don't make a profit, you will be losing money

f. Niche – What is the advantage of your company in the market/

g. PR – Public Relations- How well have you fooled the public into thinking you really care about the community?

h. Employee Concern – How well have you fooled the employees into thinking you really care about them? And if you do care a bit about them, how much money are you willing to spend on this luxury item?

ICA and Homework Assignment 2

1. Why do we need mission statements?
2. What are the components of a mission statement?
3. Why is Customer Marketing Advertising essential?
4. How should we accomplish Consumer Marketing Advertising?

Internet Resources for this lesson:

General Reference Material For All Content

http://www.askmrmovies.com

Mission Statements

Customer Marketing Advertising

Tafero's Lesson Plans of Day - Strategic Management - The External Assessment - Three

Lesson 3 – The External Assessment

1. *****External Forces 83
a. economic forces
b. social, cultural, demographic and environmental forces
c. political, governmental and legal forces
d. technological forces
e. competitive forces
2. *****Economic Forces85
a. Goods or service shift
b. Credit availability
c. Level of disposable income
d. Interest rates
e. Inflation rate
f. Government deficits
g. GDP trend
h. Consumer patterns
i. Unemployment
j. Productivity
k. Currency Value
l. Stock Market Trends
m. Foreign Economic Conditions
n. Import/Export Problems
o. Demand Shifts
p. Pricing Fluctuations
q. Tax Rates
r. Energy Needs
3. *****Social Forces – 90
a. Special Interest Groups - CCP
b. Immigration and Emigration trends
c. Per Capita Income

d. Ethics
e. Sexual Equality
f. Racial Tranquility
g. Birth Rate
h. Education Levels
i. Government Control
j. Retirement Issues
k. Environmental Concerns
l. Energy Consumption
m. Transportation Issues
n. Housing Concerns
4. *****Technological Forces93
a. Internet
b. Communication devices
c. Web Sites for Businesses – no web site, no business (you are just a store)
d. Level of Industrialization within your country
e. Level of Scientific Advancement within a country – For example, if the rest of the world's students have complete, unrestricted access to the internet and another country's students do not, then the country with limited access will be at a greater developmental and economic disadvantage.

ICA and Homework Assignments

Some External Forces Are Beyond Our Control

Write a paragraph on the following essays questions:

1. Discuss External Forces
2. Discuss Economic Forces
3. Discuss Social Forces
4. Discuss Technological Forces

Internet Resources for this lesson:

General Reference Material For All Content

http://www.askmrmovies.com

External Forces

www.knowthis.com/principles-of-marketing-tutorials/

Technological Forces

www.strategy-formulation.24xls.com/en106

Tafero's Lesson Plans of the Day - Strategic Management - The External Assessment Part Two - Four

Lesson 4 – The External Assessment – Part 2

Are You Ready For Change?

1. *****General Competition Variables96
a. Strengths
b. Weaknesses
c. Objectives
d. Response to Events
e. Vulnerability to your strategies
f. Vulnerability to our competitor's strategies
g. Positioning (Market Share)
h. Current Sales
i. Current Stock Market Price
j. Intellectual Theft and Knockoffs
2. *****Specific Competition Variables (not in book)
a. Advertising Strategies and Cost
b. Cost of Goods
c. Rent or Purchase of Land or Buildings
d. Tech capability

e. Transportation for Employees
f. Energy Costs
g. Insurance
h. Warehouse Maintenance
i. Vehicles For Transport to Retailers
j. Sales Force – Cold Callers – Inhouse (telemarketing)- Closers
k. Suppliers – Walmart and you are quite different
l. Globalization
3. *****EFE – External Factor Evaluation 109
a. List key external factors
b. Assign each factor a weight that adds up to 1
c. Assign a weight of 1-4 to the current strength of your company to each factor
d. Multiply b and c for a weighted score in each factor
e. Add the weighted scores of the factors for a Total Score

4. *****CPM – Competitive Profile Matrix 111
a. Identifies major competitors
b. Lists variables of Success Factors
c. Gives a weight to each of these factors
d. Gives a score for each of these factors
e. Compares the scores for each of the factors
f. Compares the total scores of each company
g. Allows for an Internal Analysis by strategists to see what needs improvement

ICA and HW assignments – Lesson 4

It's a Jungle Out There

Write a paragraph on each of these essay questions:

1. Discuss General Competition Variables
2. Discuss Specific Competition Variables
3. Create an EFE for Walmart (you can make up the numbers)
4. Create a CPM for Mobile Phone companies in China (3 is enough and make up the numbers)

Internet Resources for this lesson:

General Reference Material For All Content

http://www.askmrmovies.com

Internal Factor Evaluation

Competitive Profile Matrix

Tafero's Lesson Plans of the Day - Strategic Management - The Internal Assessment - Five

Lesson 5 – The Internal Assessment

This man is doing an internal assessment of the Pepperoni Pizza he had for lunch

1. *****Functions of Management131
a. Planning
b. Organizing
c. Motivating
d. Staffing
e. Controlling
2. Planning 132 – preparing for the future
3. Organizing 132 – structuring task and authority relationships
4. Motivating132 – efforts toward shaping human behavior
5. Staffing132-personnel human resource management
6. Controlling 132 – making sure results are consistent with plans – or go to B,C,D
7. *****Functions of Marketing136
a. Customer analysis 136 – targeting
b. Selling products/services136 – advertising campaigns
c. Product/service planning136 – budgets
d. Pricing136- market forces
e. Marketing research136- internet and live (R&D)
f. Distribution136 – getting your product to customers (wholesale and retail)
g. Opportunity 136 – strategic alliances, takeovers
8. *****Marketing Audit139
a. Market segmented properly?
b. Positioned well vs competitors?
c. Market share increasing?
d. Distribution reliable and cost effective?
e. Sales force sufficient?
f. Doing Market Research (R&D)?

g. Quality good?
h. Service good?
i. Priced Correctly?
j. Advertising effective?
k. Budgeting accurate?
l. Staff trained properly?

9. Current Ratio144= Current Assets over Current Liabilities
10. Debt to Total Assets Ratio144 = Total Debt over Total Assets
11. Inventory Turnover144 = Sales over Inventory of Finished goods
12. Gross Profit Margin144 = Sales-cost of goods sold over sales
13. Net Profit Margin144 = Net Income over sales
14. Return on Total Assets145 = Net Income over Total Assets
15. Stock Price145 = Assets-Liabilities over Total Shares Outstanding

ICA and HW assignments

Can you guess which one got the promotion?

Write a paragraph for each of these essay questions:

1. Discuss Functions of Management
2. Discuss Functions of Marketing
3. Discus the Marketing Audit Process
4. Discuss various Ratio formulae

Internet Resources for this lesson:

General Reference Material For All Content

http://www.askmrmovies.com

Marketing Functions

www.management-hub.com/marketing-management-roles-functions.htm

Management Functions

www.managementstudyguide.com/management_functions.htm

Tafero's Lesson Plans of the Day - Strategic Management - The Internal Assessment Part Two -Lesson Six

Lesson 6- The Internal Assessment II

This is a Poster Boy For Recent International Investment Bankers

1. *****The Finance/Accounting Audit147
a. Where is the firm strong and weak according to ratio analyses
b. Can the firm raise capital?
c. How is cash flow?
d. Are budgets relatively accurate?
e. Are dividends feasible?
f. Investor and Stockholder Confidence levels high?
g. Staff experienced and well-trained?
2. *****The Functions of Production Management147
a. Process – design of production
b. Capacity – output design
c. Inventory – how much do you want to store?
d. Workforce – staffing considerations
e. Quality – higher the quality, higher the price
f. Service – higher the service, higher the price
3. *****Production audit checklist149
a. Production components reliable and reasonable?
b. Office and Factory machinery in good condition?
c. Inventory sufficient and cost-effective lifo? fifo?
d. Do you have good location?
e. Do you have a healthy revenue producing web site?
4. *****Production Strategies150
a. Low-cost (China's favorite, but too much is dangerous)
b. High-Qualiy –mostly favored by Western Countries (also can be dangerous)
c. Customer-Focused – A good strategy in moderation
d. Rapid Product Turnover- a risky approach at best (Chinese potato chips)
e. Vertical Integration- difficult to implement (everyone working on same page)
f. Centralization – generally a good strategy for both companies and governments, but has various weaknesses.
g. Decentralization – risky approach has many weaknesses, but can be very productive if properly implemented
h. Automation – eliminating human labor is almost always a good idea, but has certain weaknesses when trying to use automation for more subtle work.
i. Employee Loyalty- in the 21st century, this is a concept that is difficult to sell to young workers; especially ones laid off during financial crises.
5. *****Research and Development Audit
a. Does company have an adequate department?
b. If outsourced, are results cost effective?

c. Are workers well trained and qualified?
d. Enough funding in budget?
e. Hardware up to date?
f. Communication between R&D department to others adequate
6. Benchmarking157 – tool for measuring your performance various standards
7. *****IFE- Internal Factor Evaluation157
a. List key internal factors
b. Assign a weight to these factors from 0 to 1. Sum must equal 1
c. Assign numbers to each factor for weaknesses 1 – minor to 4- major
d. Multiply each factor's weight by its rating to determine weighted score
e. Sum the rated scores for each variable to measure internal factors

ICA and HW assignments

Uncle Scrooge did not have an MBA

Write a paragraph on each of these essay questions:

1. Discuss the Finance/Accounting Audit.
2. Discuss the Functions of Production Management
3. Discuss the Production Audit Checklist
4. Discuss Production Strategies
5. Discuss the R&D audit
6. Construct and IFE for a company of your choice.

Internet Resources for this lesson:

General Reference Material For All Content

http://www.askmrmovies.com

Finance Strategies

www.unu.edu/unupress/unupbooks/uu29me/uu29me0a.htm

Production Strategies

www.slideshare.net

Tafero's Lesson Plans of the Day - Strategic Management - Strategies in Action - Seven

Lesson 7 – Strategies in Action

1. *****Alternatives to Not Managing by Objective170
a. XManaging by Extrapolation – just keep doing things the same way because you are making money today
b. Managing by Crisis – Handling one problem at a time without planning how to deal with them in the future.
c. Managing by Subjectives – just do the best you can in the way you think it should be done
d. Managing by Hope – the future will always be better and not worse than the present

2. *****Types of Strategies173
a. Forward integration – gaining ownership of some of your limited partners
b. Backward integration – gaining ownership of some of your suppliers
c. Horizontal integration – gaining ownership of one or more of your competitors
d. Market penetration – seeking increased market share
e. Market development – introducing old products into a new geographic area
f. Product development – improving or creating new products
g. Related diversification – adding new products related to old ones (straws for soda)
h. Unrelated diversification – adding new products unrelated to old ones (computers and food)
i. Retrenchment – also known as downsizing, it is usually the last step before bankruptcy.X
j. Divestiture – selling off part of your business that is losing money (IBM- Lenovo)X
k. Liquidation – selling off everything as you go bankruptX

3. Porter's Three Generic Strategies188
a. Cost leadership – low cost - Trustmart
b. Cost leadership – best value – Walmart
c. Differentiation – having a niche

4. *****Means For Achieving Strategies193
a. Joint ventures/partnering – usually a fixed percentage for each partner
b. Mergers – a friendly agreement to combine resources with another company
c. Acquisition – can be friendly or unfriendly depending on the economic condition of both companies
d. First to market – being the first to sell an item like IPAD Table of winners and losers on 199
e. Outsourcing – reducing costs by hiring cheaper labor in other countries (Mexico, China)

5. *****Non-Profit Organizations203
a. Educational Institutions – Jimei U, Xiamen U

b. Medical Organizations – Xiamen #2 Hospital
c. Government Agencies and Departments – CIFIT, Bureau of Foreign Investment

ICA and HW Assignments

Porter's Strategies

Write a paragraph on each essay question:

1. Discuss Alternatives to not managing by objective.
2. Discuss the many types of strategies and their meanings (2 paragraphs)
3. Discuss Porter's three generic strategies
4. Discuss Means for achieving strategies
5. Discuss non-profit organizations

Internet Resources for this lesson:

General Reference Material For All Content

http://www.askmrmovies.com

Porter's Strategies

www.quickmba.com/strategy/generic.shtml

Alternative Management Strategies

www.ncbi.nlm.nih.gov/pubmed/17138407

Tafero's Lesson Plans of the Day - Strategic Management - Strategy Analysis and Choice - Eight

Lesson 8 – Strategy Analysis and Choice

Another Example of Poor Planning Without Contingencies

1. *****The Comprehensive Strategic Management Model216
a. Develop Vision and/or Mission Statement
b. Perform Internal Audit
c. Perform External Audit
d. Establish Objectives
e. Evaluate Strategies
f. Implement Strategies
g. Controls for Strategies

2. *****The SWOT analysis221
a. List external opportunities
b. List external threats
c. List internal strengths
d. List internal weaknesses
e. Match internal strengths with external opportunities
f. Match internal weaknesses with external opportunities
g. Match internal strengths with external threats
h. Match internal weaknesses with external threats

3. *****The Quantitative Strategic Planning Matrix- Components241
External Factors
a. Economy
b. Political/Government/Legal
c. Social/Demographic
d. Tech
e. Competitive
       Internal Factors
a. Management
b. Marketing/Sales/Advertising/WebSite
c. Finance/Accounting
d. Production
e. R&D
f. Information Systems (Tech/WebSite)

4. *****The QSPM Steps-241
a. Make a list of external opportunities and threats in left column
b. Make a list of internal strengths and weaknesses in left column with A
c. Assign weights to each external and internal factor

d. Find Possible Matching strategies
e. Determine the Attractiveness Scores
f. Compute the Total Attractiveness Score
g. Compute the Sum Total Attractiveness Score

ICA and HW Assignment

1. Discuss Comprehensive Strategic Management
2. Do a SWOT analysis of your own company
3. Do a QSPM for your own company
4. How does SWOT differ from a CPM?

Internet Resources for this lesson:

General Reference Material For All Content

http://www.askmrmovies.com

Comprehensive Strategic Management
www.scribd.com/doc/.../The-Nature-of-Strategic-Management

SWOT Analysis
www.quickmba.com/strategy/swot/

Tafero's Lesson Plans of the Day - Strategic Management - Implementing Strategy - Nine

Lesson 9 – Implementing Strategies

1. *****Contrasting Strategy Formulation and Strategy Implementation262
a. Formulation positions forces before the action
b. Implementation manages the forces during the action
c. Formulation focuses on effectiveness
d. Implementation focuses on efficiency
e. Formulation is primarily an intellectual process
f. Implementation is primarily an operational process
g. Formulation requires good intuition and analytical skills
h. Implementation requires motivation and leadership skills
i. Formulation requires coordination among a few individuals
j. Implementation requires coordination among many individuals
2. *****Annual Objectives264
a. A basis for allocating resources
b. A mechanism for evaluating managers
c. Monitor progress toward long range goals
d. Establish organizational and department priorities
3. *****Company Policies267
a. Offer workshops and seminars or limited development?
b. Recruitment from agencies, campuses, or newspapers?
c. Promote within or hire from outside?
d. Compensation for long term or short term objectives?
e. Amount of employee benefits?
f. Negotiate directly or indirectly with unions?
g. Delegation thru decentralization or authority from centralized location
h. Overtime and how much?
i. High or low inventory stock?
j. One or more suppliers?
k. Buy, rent or lease buildings, equipment?
l. How much quality?
m. Many or few production standards (same as quality control)
n. One, two or three shifts?
4. *****Chandler's Strategy Structure Relationship270
a. New Strategy is Formulated – (PLAN A)
b. PLAN A fails
c. Organizational results lag
d. New Organizational structure is established to correct Plan A
e. Organizational results improve

f. As a result of new structuring PLAN B is formulated
g. Process is continuous on a DAILY or WEEKLY basis

Lesson 9 ICA - Homework Essays

1. Discuss the differences between strategy formulation and implementation
2. Discuss the problems with Annual Objectives
3. Discuss the debates of Company Policies
4. Discuss Chandler's Strategy Formulation

Internet Resources for this lesson:

General Reference Material For All Content

http://www.askmrmovies.com

Annual Objectives

www.businessweek.com/.../define_annual_objectives_with_your_team.html

Chandler's Strategy

www.provenmodels.com/7

Tafero's Lesson Plans of Day - Strategic Management - Implementation Strategies (PartTwo) - Ten

Lesson 10 – Continuation of Implementation Strategies

1. *****The Strategic Business Unit274
a. Chief Executive Officer (CEO)- Strategic Manager
b. Chief Strategic Officer (CSO)
c. Chief Finance Officer (CFO) – Accounting Manager
d. Chief Operating Officer (COO) – Factory Manager
e. Chief Information Officer (CIO) – Web Site Coordinator and Research Manager*
• Giving both of these important functions to the same person can be very dangerous; the chance that one task will be done and the other neglected will be very high. It is recommended that TWO people with two distinct titles be given for these two functions.
f. VP of Human Resources – Personnel Director
g. VP of Marketing – (Sales and Advertising Director)*
• Giving both of these important functions to the same person can be very dangerous; the chance that one task will be done and the other neglected will be very high. It is recommended that TWO people with two distinct titles be given for these two functions. The upper elements of the SBU usually are referred to as the Board of Trustees and the CEO is usually the Chairperson of this group.
2. *****Marketing Issues 306
a. Exclusive or Multiple distributors?
b. Heavy, Light or No TV advertising?
c. Exclusive customer benefits or not?
d. Price Leader or Follower?
e. Complete or Limited Warranty (Quality)?
f. Sales professionals paid on straight commission or salary/commission?
g. Advertising online primary revenue stream or not?

3. *****Elements of Market Segmentation309
a. Geographic – region, province, city, size, density, climate
b. Demographic – age, gender, family size, income, occupation, education, religion, race, nationality
c. Psychographic – social class, personality
d. Behavioral – usage, benefit sought, user status, user rate, loyalty status, readiness, attitude

4. *****Positioning311
a. Select criteria or benchmarks of the industry
b. Map your competition according to various variables: personal /impersonal, aggressive/passive with two dimensions and an axis at a time

c. Look for vacant or scarcely populated areas
d. Develop a Plan A to position your company in that vacant or scarcely populated area

ICA - HW 10 – Four Essays

1. Discuss the Strategic Business Unit
2. Discuss Marketing Issues
3. Discuss Elements of Market Segmentation
4. Discuss Positioning

Internet Resources for this lesson:

General Reference Material For All Content

http://www.askmrmovies.com

Positioning
www.learnmarketing.net/positioning.htm

Strategic Business Units

www.gavrielshaw.com/.../business.../strategic-business-units/

Lesson 11 – Midterm Paper and/or Exam

Tafero's Lesson Plans of Day - Strategic Management – Control Strategies - Twelve

Lesson 12 – Control Strategies

1. *****Finance/Accounting Issues313
a. Raise capital with short-term debt, long-term debt, preferred stock or common stock?
b. Lease or buy fixed assets?
c. Use LIFO or FIFO?
d. Extend Accounts Receivable Times and Penalties? Discounts?
e. How much cash on hand for operating expenses and potential takeovers or mergers?

2. *****Projected Financial Statement Analysis318
a. Income Statement – sales minus cost of goods sold= gross margin minus additional expenses of selling = net income
b. Projected Balance Sheet – Assets minus Liabilities = 0 or shows a loss to avoid paying taxes

3. *****R&D Issues325
a. Emphasize product or process improvement?
b. Stress basic or applied research?
c. Be a leader or follower in R&D?
d. Develop robotics or manual labor?
e. Spend high, medium or low $ on R&D?
f. Perform R&D internally or contract externally?
g. Use academics or private-sector researchers?

4. *****Web Site Issues (not in book)
a. Should you create a web site?
b. Should it be just a few pages, cover all of sales, or be massive and cover the entire company?
c. Should it be the primary or secondary revenue stream or have no revenue?
d. Should you spend a small, medium or large amount of money on your site?
e. Should control of the site be in the hands of technicians or the CEO and Board of Trustees?
ICA - HW 12 – Four Essays

1. Discuss Finance and Accounting Issues
2. Discuss Projected Financial Statement Analysis
3. Discuss R&D Issues.
4. Discuss Web Sites.

Internet Resources for this lesson:

General Reference Material For All Content

http://www.askmrmovies.com

Finance

www.google.com/finance

R&D

www.investopedia.com

Lesson 13 – Strategy Review, Evaluation and Control (Moving on to Plan B)

1. *****Strategy Bases340
A. How have competitors reacted to our strategies?
B. How have competitors strategies changed?
C. How have competitors strengths and weaknesses changed?
D. Why are competitors making certain strategic changes?
E. Why are some competitor's strategies more successful than others?
F. How much should we cooperate with our competitors?

2. *****Measuring Internal and External Strengths and Weaknesses341
a. Are our internal strengths currently strong?
b. Have we added additional internal strengths? What are they?
c. Do we still have the same Internal Weaknesses? To Whatdegree?
d. What are our current external opportunities?
e. What are our current external threats?

3. *****Measuring Organizational Performance343
a. Return on Investment (how much did you invest and how much do you have now?)
b. Return on Equity (how much is your share when you invested andhow much is it now?)
c. Profit Margin (how much do you make on every dollar invested?)
d. Market Share – (how much of the market do you control?)
e. Debt to Equity – (How much do you own minus how much you owe?)
f. Earnings Per Share – (How much of the profits do you want to show in your Stock Price?)
g. Sales Growth –(How much have your sales increased or decreased over a specific period of time?)
h. Asset Growth (how much have your assets increased or decreased over a specific period of time?)

4. *****Contingency Planning (Plan B and Beyond)351
a. Identify favorable and unfavorable events that threaten Plan A (monthly, quarterly, yearly)
b. Calculate when or where these events will occur and try to factor them in Plan A
c. Assess the impact of each of these events and try to factor the impact into Plan A
d. Develop Plan B, C and D based on these new assessments
e. Be prepared to develop Plan B as soon as possible to incorporate the useful elements of Plan A
f. Be prepared to make this process a CONTINUOUS one which needs periodical modification.

ICA – HW - Essay Questions for Lesson 13

1. Discuss Strategy Bases.
2. Discuss Measuring Internal and External Forces
3. Discuss Measuring Organizational Performance
4. Discuss Contingency Plans (Plan B,C,D etc)

Internet Resources for this lesson:

General Reference Material For All Content

http://www.askmrmovies.com

Strategy Bases

www.oup.com/uk/orc/bin/9780199288304/henry_ch05.pdf

Contingency Plans

www.factoidz.com/strategic-management-and-planning-the-tafero-principle-...

Lesson 14 – Field Practicum; Drawbacks to case studies in American Texts

A. Almost all case studies in books before 2008 are pre-Global Financial Crisis, so they have little value as a current analytical tool. Most of them are five or more years old. That is before the advent of a great deal of technology and the changing of a number of business practices.

B. Almost all of them are American Companies, so they have little value to the 99% of the international students who will be working for international companies. A few case studies of companies like Lenovo, Alibaba and China Mobile might be far more useful in the future.

C. Suggested Field Practicum

1. Development and Review of Resume
2. Exhaustive Research on Company of Practicum Before Fieldwork
3. Creation of a Portfolio for Company of Practicum, including research data and advertising materials
4. A carefully constructed IFE
5. A carefully constructed EFE
6. A carefully constructed CPM
7. A carefully constructed SWOT
8. An analysis of the market share and reasons for gain or loss
9. An analysis of sales and reasons for gain or loss
10. An analysis of the stock market price and reasons for gain or loss
11. A ppt presentation containing all of the above.
12. A strategic plan for the company to obtain or keep 8,9 and 10..
13. Interview practices
14. On-the-job hands on experiences to be kept in journal – minimal details
15. On site inspection of progress twice a semester
16. Final journal submission

ICA-HW essay questions

MBA Field Study Students

1. How can a portfolio of what you can do in advertising for a private company give you an edge at the interview?
2. How can a presentation of your preferred company's market share, sales and stock market price with a short analysis of a suggested course of action give you another edge at your interview?
3. What separates the thousands of interviewees in business from the few dozen who are really prepared to take on the new job?

4. Why are old-fashioned concepts of the interview process practically a guarantee that you will be getting a second-tier or third tier job with a company (if you get hired at all).

Internet Resources for this lesson:

General Reference Material For All Content

http://www.askmrmovies.com

Business Portfolios

www.ehow.com/business-portfolios

Interview and Portfolios

www.mastercareercounselor.blogspot.com/.../business-portfolio-how-import...

Part two of this book is a course overview on Leadership.

Tafero's Lesson Plan of Day - Leadership - The Importance of Leadership - One

Lesson 1 – The Importance of Leadership

1. Leadership 2 – Social influence through ideas and deeds
2. The Three Types of Leaders 3
a. Teachers - creativity
b. Heroes – great causes
c. Rulers – domination of others
3. Short List of leaders
a. Aristotle - t
b. Plato - t
c. Laozi - t
d. Confucius - t
e. Buddha - t
f. Gandhi - h
g. Jesus - t
h. Muhummad - t
i. Moses - h
j. Marx - t
k. Alexander - r
l. Luther - h
m. Charlemagne - r
n. Genghis Khan - r
o. Einstein - t
p. DaVinci - t
q. Julius Caesar - r
r. Saladin - r
s. Mao Zedong – r

4. How do leaders learn?
a. Experience 6 – experience is the best teacher for leaders according to the US Chamber of Commerce
b. Examples 6 – examples or models is the second source for most developing leaders according to the US Chamber of Commerce.
c. Books and School 6 – these are the third most important elements of learning according to the US Chamber of Commerce.
5. What do people want in a leader? 6
a. Integrity and honesty
b. Job knowledge
c. People-building skills
6. What gives leaders satisfaction? 9

a. Power
b. Helping
c. High Income
d. Respect and Status
e. Opportunity
f. Knowledge
g. Control
7. What frustrates leaders? 9
a. Uncompensated work time
b. Numerous problems
c. Not enough authority
d. Loneliness
e. Organizational Politics
f. Conflicting Goals
g. People Problems
8. Primary Concerns of Leaders 10
a. Tasks
b. People
Leaders vary by their emphasis on one and the secondary nature of another. This behavior has two very different outcomes. Primary concern for the task tends to subjugate treatment of people. Primary concern for people tends to subjugate the completion of a task.
9. Key Areas of Leadership 12
a. The leadership equation – qualities of leaders, followers and situations
b. Power of vision – direction
c. Ethics – leading with morals
d. Empowerment – democratic leadership
e. Leadership principles – winning teams
f. Understanding people – psychology
g. Multiplying effectiveness – efficiency
h. Developing others – teaching
i. Performance management – discipline

ICA and HW 1

Answer the following essay questions:

1. How do leaders learn?
2. How are leaders selected by the people?
3. How does a leader solve the problem of putting people or tasks first?
4. Discuss the key areas of leadership.

Internet Resources for this lesson:

General Reference Material For All Content

http://www.askmrmovies.com

Leadership
www.nwlink.com/~donclark/leader/leader.html

Task or People?
www.changefactory.com.au/leadership-is-it-better-to-be-people-or-task-or...

Suggested Film: Spartacus

Tafero's Lesson Plans of Day - Leadership - The Leadership Equation - Two

Lesson 2 – The Leadership Equation

Brand Leadership Equation

1. Three Types of Leadership Behavior 20
a. Autocratic or dictatorial
b. Democratic or group
c. Laissez-faire or passive monitoring such as in financial markets

2. Two results of Leadership Behavior 20
a. Job-centered results
b. Employee-centered results
Of these two results, the job-centered results are, by far, the most common

3. Five Major Styles of Management 20-21
a. Impoverished manager – low concern for the job and low concern for workers (c type)
b. Sweatshop manager – high concern for job, low concern for workers (a type)
c. Country club manager – high concern for people, low concern for job (b type)
d. Status Quo manager – manages exactly like predecessor; moderate concern (b type)

e. The Fully Functioning Manager - High concern for production and high concern for people; workaholic (b type)

f. The Paternalistic Manager – Uses $ and promotions for compliance and loyalty

g. Opportunistic Manager – uses any of the major styles needed to advance one's career

4. Contingency Theory – 25 – that leadership qualities vary from situation to situation.

5. Transformational Leadership – 27 – Weber believes that extraordinary people (like Lawrence of Arabia, Spartacus, Muhammad, Jesus) inspire others and bring forth great loyalty.

ICA and HW 2

Answer the essay questions below.

1. Discuss transformational leadership.
2. Discuss various styles of management.
3. Discuss the Contingency Theory.
4. Discuss types of leadership behavior.

Internet Resources for this lesson:

General Reference Material For All Content

http://www.askmrmovies.com

Contingency Theory
www.businessmate.org/Article.php?ArtikelId=11

Transformational Leadership

www.leadingtoday.org/.../transformationalleadership.htm

 Suggested Film: King of Kings

Tafero's Lesson Plans of Day - Leadership - Leadership Qualities and Situation Factors - Three

Lesson 3 – Leadership Qualities and Characteristics of Followers

Confucius

1. Major Qualities of Leadership 30-31

a. Vision
b. Ability
c. Enthusiasm
d. Stability
e. Concern for Others
f. Self-Confidence
g. Persistence
h. Vitality
i. Charisma
j. Integrity

2. Withholding Trust 37
a. Breakdown of family structure
b. Decline of social structures
c. Lack of shared values and sense of community
d. Discovery of violated trust by previous leaders

3. Principles of Trust 37-38
a. Deal openly with everyone
b. Consider all points of view
c. Keep Promises
d. Give Responsibilities (Delegation of Authority)
e. Listen to Understand
f. Care about People

4. Trust – 41 – Four levels of Trust
a. Cynic – trusts almost no one
b. Skeptic – trusts very few
c. Guarded Trust – trusts many, reserves judgment
d. Trusting – trusts almost all

(have class do Trust test on 39)

ICA and HW 3

Answer these essay questions

1. Discuss the four levels of trust.
2. Discuss the principles of trust.
3. Why do people withhold trust?
4. Discuss the major qualities of leadership.

Internet Resources for this lesson:

General Reference Material For All Content

http://www.askmrmovies.com

Qualities of Leadership

www.focus.com/briefs/human-resources/top-10-leadership-qualities/

Trust
www.businessweek.com/magazine/.../b4145076753447.htm

Suggested Film: Siddhartha

Lesson 4 – Situational Factors

The 300 Spartans were surrounded and greatly outnumbered, but still did well.

1. Leader-Follower Compatibility 43
a. Size of Organization
b. Social and Psychological Climate
c. Type, Place, and Purpose of Task

2. Types of Intelligence 49
a. Verbal
b. Musical
c. Logical
d. Visual-Spatial
e. Physical Body
f. Intrapersonal – (Introspective) – Understand Yourself
g. Interpersonal – Understand Others

3. Styles of Leadership according to various researchers: 53
a. Modeling yourself from others
b. Individuals usually prefer the same model of leading and following; this sometimes causes confusion at one level or another.
c. All three basic types of leadership (dictatorial, democratic and free-reign) have all been successful with various leaders at one time or another (Elizabeth I, Jefferson, Eisenhower respectively)
d. There is no universally effective style of leadership since all three basic types have been successful on numerous occasions.

4. Problems in Conflict Resolution in Leading 55
a. Decision-Making
b. Goal-Setting
c. Communication

ICA and HW 4

Texans at the Alamo were almost in the same situation as the 300 Spartans

Answer the following essay questions

1. Discuss problems of conflict in leadership.
2. Discuss effective styles of leadership.
3. Discuss the various types of intelligence.
4. Discuss Leader-Follower Capability.

Internet Resources for this lesson:

General Reference Material For All Content

http://www.askmrmovies.com

Types of Intelligence
www.skyview.vansd.org/.../The%20Nine%20Types%20of%20Intelligence.html

Leader-Follower Capabilities
www.leadmcg.com/success/index

Suggested Film: Gandhi

Tafero's Lesson Plans of Day - Leadership - Vision - Five

Lesson 5 – The Importance of Vision

1. Elements of Organizational Success 61
a. Vision
b. Skills
c. Incentives
d. Resources
e. Action Plan

2. Possible Results without one of the key variables 61
a. Organizational Success
b. Confusion (without vision)
c. Anxiety and mixed results (without skills)
d. Gradual change or inertia (without incentives)
e. Frustration (without resources or money)
f. False Starts (without a good plan)

3. The Three Act Process for Change 63
a. Recognize Need for Change (Global Financial Crisis)
b. Create a Clear and Positive Vision for the Future (Never Let it Happen Again)
c. Institute Empowering Structures and Processes to Achieve the Vision (create laws and rules to never let it happen again)

4. Other Elements of Leadership 63

a. Leadership is important at every level of the organization
b. Positions and titles have little or no relationship to leadership
c. Without leadership, organizations falter
d. Interdependence is better than individualism in Organizational Leadership
e. Good leadership inspires others to perform tasks
f. Leadership requires understanding by subordinates

5. The Concepts of Vision 67

a. Initiate
b. Realistic Challenge
c. Seek Early Involvement
d. Encourage Widespread Comment
e. Maintain Communication
f. Allow some time for process to work
g. Demonstrate Commiment
h. Maintain Harmony

6. Other Content of Vision 67-68
a. Central Purpose
b. Broad Goal
c. Core Values
d. Stakeholders
e. SWOT analysis
f. Strategic Initiatives
g. Tactical Plans

ICA and HW 5

Answer the following essay questions

1. Discuss concepts and content of vision.
2. Discuss the three-act process for change.
3. Discuss the negative results of management without vision.
4. Discuss the elements of organizational success.

Internet Resources for this lesson:

General Reference Material For All Content

http://www.askmrmovies.com

Vision
www.quickmba.com/strategy/vision/

Three-Act Process for Change

www.delta7.com/delta7-change-process-stage3-act/

Suggested Film: Lawrence of Arabia

Tafero's Lesson Plans of Day - Leadership - Motive and Ethics - Six

- Lesson 6 – The Motive to Lead and Organizational Climate

Julius Caesar

1. Basic motives for Leadership 72
a. Power
b. Achievement
c. Affiliation – helping others

2. Elements of a supportive organizational climate 77
a. Reward Systems
b. Clarity of Goals
c. High Standards
d. Support
e. Leadership

3. Patterns of Leadership 81
a. Exploitive – autocratic and non-participatory-dictatorships
b. Impovished – primarily autocratic and non-participatory, but with some participation of workers
c. Supportive – primarily democratic and participatory, but with mixed agendas
d. Enlightened – democratic and participatory with a clear agenda

4. Principles of an Enlightened Organization 82
a. Human resources are the organization's greatest asset
b. Every individual is treated with understanding, dignity, warmth and support
c. Use vision and team building
d. Set high performance goals at every level of the organization

5. Conditions for Community Building 83-84
a. Shared vision
b. Incorporate diversity
c. Shared culture
d. Internal Communication
e. Consideration and Trust
f. Maintenance
g. Participation
h. Development
i. Affirmation – convincing itself it is doing a good job
j. Links with outside groups

ICA and HW 7
Answer the following essay questions

1. Discuss the conditions for community building.
2. Discuss patterns of leadership.
3. Discuss elements of a supportive organizational climate.
4. Discuss basic motives for leadership

Internet Resources for this lesson:

General Reference Material For All Content

http://www.askmrmovies.com

Community Building

Leadership Motives

 Suggested Film – Julius Caesar

Lesson 7 – Leadership Ethics

1. Moral Development – 97
a. Associations –family, friends and role models
b. Books – knowledge and reading
c. Self-Concept – what we think of ourselves
d. Visual Media – how we are affected by film and TV
e. Internet and Cell Phone persona – our communications personality

2. Levels of Moral Development – 99
a. Pre-conventional Morality – punishment/pleasure
b. Conventional Morality – group conformity
c. Post-conventional Morality – Judgment based on what we believe to be right or wrong

3. The Heinz Reasoning Arguments for stealing drugs 99

a. Punishment-go to jail/Pleasure – I keep my wife and can be happy
b. Conventional – most people don't steal drugs/most people will do anything for their wives
c. Post-Conventional – I will steal the drugs because I think the law is unjust and my wife is more important than any law/as a law-abiding citizen, I must respect the property of others and the laws of the land

4. Ingredients for Moral Leadership 104
a. Motives – why should I do this- because it is the right thing to do
b. Means – do you have the means to do something about a problem?
c. Consequences – do you consider what will happen if you do or do not do something?

ICA and HW 7
Answer the following essay questions

1. Discuss the ingredients for Moral Leadership
2. Discuss the Heinz Reasoning Arguments for stealing drugs
3. Discuss Levels of Moral Development
4. Discuss the Elements of Moral Development

Internet Resources for this lesson:

General Reference Material For All Content

http://www.askmrmovies.com

Heinz Reasoning

Levels of Moral Development

Suggested Film: Lincoln

Tafero's Lesson Plans of Day - Leadership - Values and Ethics at Work - Eight

Lesson 8 – The Role of Values

1. Value Problems 106
a. Lack of understanding
b. Differences in value systems
c. Receiving mixed messages
d. Disorganization
e. Discontent
f. Insensitivity

2. Values in the American Workplace 107
a. Honesty
b. Respect
c. Service
d. Excellence
e. Integrity

3. Western Traditional Definitions of Good and Right 107-109
a. If you have power, then you must be good
b. If you have integrity then you are good
c. If you have natural simplicity then you are good
d. If you are doing the will of God then you are good
e. If something gives you pleasure then it must be good
f. If most people benefit from something it must be good
g. If something is practical it must be good

4. Full-Swing Values 111
a. Know one's values
b. Cherish one's values
c. Declare one's values
d. Act on one's values
e. Act habitually on one's values

ICA and HW 8
Answer the following essay questions

1. Discuss full-swing values
2. Discuss Western tradition definitions of good
3. Discuss values in the American workplace
4. Discuss value problems

Internet Resources for this lesson:

General Reference Material

http://www.askmrmovies.com

American Workplace Values

Western Tradition Definitions of Good

Suggested Film: Norma Rae

Lesson 9 – Ethics at Work

1. Work Rules 128
a. Government relations
b. Employee relations
c. Community relations
d. Business relations
e. Production rules
f. Consumer relations

2. Ethics of successful companies 128
a. Try to satisfy all of their constituencies –customers, employees owners, suppliers dealers, communities and governments
b. They are dedicated to high and broad values
c. They are committed to learning
d. They try to be the best at whatever they do

3. Four basic questions of ethics 129
a. Is it the truth?
b. Is it fair for all concerned?
c. Will it build goodwill or better relationships?
d. Will it be beneficial to all concerned?

4. Cost of Ethical Misconduct 129
a. Loss of customers and sales
b. Increased turnover
c. Demoralization
d. Loss of equity
e. High operating costs of penalties
f. Legal expenses
g. Lender costs
h. Loss of public trust
i. Failure of the enterprise

ICA and HW 9

Answer the following essay questions

1. Discuss the costs of ethical misconduct.
2. Discuss the four basic questions of ethics.
3. Discuss the ethics of successful companies.
4. Discuss work rules.

Internet Resources for this lesson:

General Reference Materials

http://www.askmrmovies.com

Ethics of successful companies

Four Basic Questions of Ethics

Suggested Film: Tucker

www.ingramcontent.com/pod-product-compliance
Lightning Source LLC
Chambersburg PA
CBHW071728170526
45165CB00005B/2205